ONE SPRING MORE

ONE SPRING MORE

By

THOMAS GRISSOM

SUNSTONE
PRESS

SANTA FE

Sunstone books may be purchased for educational, business, or sales promotional use.
For information please write: Special Markets Department, Sunstone Press,
P.O. Box 2321, Santa Fe, New Mexico 87504-2321.

Cover design › Vicki Ahl
Printed on acid-free paper
∞

Library of Congress Cataloging-in-Publication Data

Grissom, Thomas, 1940-
  [Poems. Selections]
  One spring more : poems / by Thomas Grissom.
    pages ; cm.
  ISBN 978-0-86534-940-7 (softcover : alk. paper)
  I. Title.
  PS3607.R577O54 2013
  811'.6–dc23
                                    2013003748

WWW.SUNSTONEPRESS.COM
SUNSTONE PRESS / POST OFFICE BOX 2321 / SANTA FE, NM 87504-2321 /USA
(505) 988-4418 / ORDERS ONLY (800) 243-5644 / FAX (505) 988-1025

This Book Is For My Parents:
Annie Laura and John Woodrow

Many red devils ran from my heart
And out upon the page.
They were so tiny
The pen could mash them.
And many struggled in the ink.
It was strange
To write in this red muck
Of things from my heart.

Stephen Crane

Who can write entirely with unadulterated com-
passion? All prose, all poetry, to the extent that it
is not compassion, is failure.

R. D. Laing

CONTENTS

Heed the Voices of Anger

INTRODUCTION

Viewed all together, these are poems of survival. They reflect what was happening to me at the time, what was on my mind. There was no intentional unifying theme expressed in the writing of these poems beyond the cross-currents of events that make up the life of each of us. There are glimpses of the past interwoven in the present, just as there are in every life, just as what happens next is inescapably the result of all that has gone before. And in that sense they represent for me a point of departure, an attempt of sorts to look to the future. What I feel in doing so — what anyone today must feel — is a disquieting apprehension.

Ours is assuredly a time of unbridled excess spawned by unparalleled technological achievement and sophistication. Life, birth, and death are pursued headlong on a scale of such obscene distortion as to emasculate our lives of all meaning, much as if the species were in the frenzied throes of self-destruction. If we are to survive, then the illusion of an ineluctable progress and the mentality that gives rise to its unquestioned, almost instinctual, pursuit must be balanced by a different concept of himself that modern man has yet to embrace. The old values are suspect and potentially suicidal. If there has been a theme to my thoughts during the past few months, perhaps it has been simply this — I have come to believe that the greater measure of man for the future lies in what he refuses to do than in any of his accomplishments. To the degree that we are incapable of such restraint, the outcome remains uncertain and the illusion of progress may one day become the reality of extinction.

Some will note the anger they hear expressed in my poems. To this I must confess a certain guilt. Above all, poetry should reflect the inner feelings of the writer, truthfully, without regard to whether those feelings will either please or displease any other person. It is in that spirit that the initial act of disclosure is conceived, and the work remains true only to the extent that it adheres to the source of its inspiration.

Yet it is not a vindictive anger, but one born of love. Two thousand years ago Lucretius wrote *De Rerum Natura* to free men from fear and today we are more troubled than ever. The course the Greeks embarked upon and Lucretius set down for us, to seek peace and tranquility through understanding, we now recognize as delusion and it is difficult not to be angry. Still, it is love that makes us cry out, for to remain silent is not to care. Even Jeffers who could admonish us to . . .

> *Be angry at the sun for setting*
> *If these things anger you . . .*

nevertheless felt the same. It is the compassionate anger of one who feels too deeply for complacency. I offered my apologies earlier in the lines of another poem . . .

> *If what you find here troubles*
> *At least that wasn't my intent,*
> *And any harshness you may hear*
> *More for me than you was meant.*

Casita del Arroyo
Albuquerque

There is no reason
        for bitterness
                more compelling
than that for charity,
        no storm
                stays for long
the sun,
        not right or wrong
                but only time
prevails,
        no regret at death—
                life
though undeserved
        was a gift
                freely given.

The Gift She Early Gave to Me

.

THE GIFT SHE EARLY GAVE TO ME

The darkly dappled duns of spring muffle a
Woman's weaning sobs that stain with alkaline
Lace the mirrored masks reflected round
Her speechless sorrow, shrieking still across
The gape of gnawing years to mold my mind
In moribund pain—perhaps to strike me dumb
For silence softly spent in soul's repast
When lilting-laughtered games with shadowed moths
Through sweet magnolia scents would not suffice.
By brighter bells she spoke the earthly coarsened
Tones that tolled the fates of decent folk
To one alive in less imperfect worlds and
Shaped me from the common clay that crumbles
Under grinding heel in disarray
Unprincipled, till hardened to insensate
Stone it finally breaks and shatters in
Discordant sounds the senses suffer to
Escape in absolution lightly laved.
And spirits flowed from fecund fields and lands
That lavished servitude upon those hapless
Held in bondage ill of their own choosing,
Who best the farrowed fetters chained them knew
Blankly without hate or love that lately
Lonely voices raise to fearful ears,
To infuse my soul with fertile seeds that one
Day grew to claim the soil of thought and deed

With noisy clamor out of context like
The child the sounds it sends to show the world
The life it briefly reckons then rescinds.
With ever steady touch she gentled febrile
Brow against the tumult raged within, till
Calmed in contemplation upon seas of
Tranquil truths I cherished secrets of
The heavens reflected in those depths, then peering
Deeper in my languorous labor found
The image everywhere the same my own,
And storms that tossed the troubled seas then
    brought
To life a sweeter taste it had not known
And swept me from my task ashore to stroll
Again in light and dappled duns of springs
The wanning winters wield, now proudly mantled
By the cloak of years that gentler sends
The knell of sheltered sounds and gives at last
To her the gift she early gave to me.

THE DELTA:

Not the accretion of alluvial deposits by which
The river at its mouth inexorably extends
The boundaries of the land slowly oceanward
But the fertile crescent stretching roughly
From Memphis to Vicksburg and lying between
The river on one side and the plateau of the
Mississippi hill country rising abruptly on the other;
The ancient alluvial flood plain of the river
Overflowing its banks each spring to spread inland
And deposit its burden of new rich black soil
On the deepening layers of earth gradually
Accumulated in this manner from time immemorial,
Overflowing each year even as the land was being
Transformed from forests and swamps to clearings
And farms and homesteads to the final cohesiveness
Of civilization with settlements and towns, and from
The dominion of the red men who first possessed
It without ever owning it to the first white settlers
Who owned it in a sense that the Indian had not
Without wanting to possess it or be possessed by it,
To the farmers and later plantation owners whose
Proprietorship was absolute to those who have
Finally made of it a commodity of no more import
Than any other of the material possessions by which
Men can accumulate and measure their wealth,
Overflowing for the final devastating time in 1927
And covering then almost the whole of the Delta

Before the waters at last receded and men began
Constructing the mound-shaped earthen levee fifty
     feet
High and three hundred feet wide at the base
That extends in places several miles from the
Main channel alongside both banks of the river
Between St. Louis and New Orleans; except along
The perimeter where it merges with the hill country
The land perfectly flat in every direction, as flat
As the bottom of the broad shallow muddy lake
That spawned and perennially nourished it, with soil
So black that a freshly turned furrow glistens
In the sunlight as though wet and so rich
That it will grow cotton higher than a man's head
And corn taller than a man on horseback, covered
Once with thick impenetrable tangles of cane
And briar and vast towering stands of dense virgin
Forests of oak and hickory and walnut and pecan,
Ash and elm and beech and maple, sweetgum and
Sycamore, poplar and magnolia and tupelo and
     dogwood,
Locust and cypress, which the white settlers most
Recently from Tennessee and Carolina and Virginia
And Georgia but ultimately from the highlands
     and moors
Of Scotland and England and from the farms and
Villages of France and Germany felled and burned to
Clear the land, themselves dispossessed and
     dispossessing

In their turn the Indians who occupied the land
Before them only to be subsequently dispossessed
In turn by the eventual inevitable subdivision of the
Land into quarter- and half-acre plots of ground
Too small for anything but the cheap, jerry-built
Houses erected on them with little hope of surviving
The term of the mortgage held by someone else with
No interest in the land beyond its sole value as a
Commodity, and by the final ineluctable emergence
Of a society which largely lives and works and plays
In towns and cities and knows no deep or
Lasting attachment to the land; the land mostly
Cleared now and growing still cotton and corn
But also rice and soybeans and pastures, oats and
Wheat and sorghum, and in the future yet other
Crops as the families remaining on the soil
Struggle to retain their precarious hold against
The gradual persistent infringement of towns and
The factories they spawn turning out perpetual
Streams of products to feed the mindless insatiable
Appetite for more and more material goods of ever-
Diminishing necessity and questionable value;
    the bear
And panther and wolf vanished forever from forests
Made too small to offer sanctuary against the
Relentless encroachment of man, but the countryside
Dotted throughout with vestiges of thickets and
Woodlots teeming with squirrels and rabbits and
Quail and in the bigger woods white-tailed deer

And turkey and wild boar flourishing in the
Second-growth timber and in the cultivated land
Along the woods' edge, and each fall streaming
Flocks of migrating ducks and geese returning along
The flyway of the great river to find shelter and
Food in flooded woods and harvested fields of grain,
But these also greatly diminished from the flocks
That once swarmed the morning skies flying from
The roost in search of food each dawn on wingbeats
That heralded with thunder the promise of a new
Day and returning each evening to choruses of
Uncoordinated cackles attesting the success of
The day's foraging, and the last undeniable
Symbol of wilderness in a land now thoroughly
Tamed the few remaining remnants of deep woods
Still standing sheltered and secluded behind the
Earthen levee alongside the ageless river; the land
Criss-crossed with roads of gravel and asphalt
And concrete running perfectly straight and neatly
Laid out on one-mile centers linking cities and
Towns with names like Tunica and Tupelo and
Indianola, Boyle and Shelby and Clarksdale,
Shaw and Inverness and Benoit, names born of
The Indian and English and Scottish and French
Heritage on which each was founded, each today
A community divided against itself with both
Sides fearful of the aspirations and the needs and
The hopes and the dreams of the other in a drama
Which began as soon as the first slave had earned

His freedom back even before they all had been freed
And bought a wife and made for himself a home
Which later became by turns a family, a settlement,
A community and a way of life to be handed down
Generation to generation, and which drama may
        never
Be finished but to whatever extent it can will be
Contested and struggled and lived and resolved
In these towns and cities against the backdrop of
This land known to all alike as simply the Delta.

THE GOLDEN ANNIVERSARY

i) Patriarchal

The graying head now is sometimes bowed as
The stooped form moves slowly on its accustomed
Rounds between house and yard and barn,
Patiently doing whatever he can do,
No more than a memory of years past.
The pastures grow taller between mowings
Than before, the leaves pile up on the roof, the lawn
Sprouts dandelions—for in these he is at the mercy
Of others. The fierce blue eyes are dimmed
And grope in shadows. The still powerful shoulders
Tell a quarter of a lifetime and his best years
Spent on crutches, in pain. At times
The hands grow frustrated, the expression
Resigned. But the face is clear
The sharp nose and stern features still
Softened by the easy smile of one
Who has always viewed the compromises of life
As bargains of his own making. There is no bitterness
And little regret. In this lies his strength.

In his life he has found some answers
Though some remain a mystery that like most
He does not easily confess or simply no longer
Ponders, content at last to leave that to others;
He will live out the remaining days at peace

In his mind—it is little enough to ask. Evenings
By the fire where before he would read he sits in
Drawing darkness and dreams, remembering a life
    lived
Simply and honestly, doing whatever had to be done
Not intentionally hurting anyone and mostly unaware
When he did; those who recall remember him as
A friend. He thinks too of days to come and
Things he will yet do before he is finished. For
He will not "go gentle into that good night," but
When he must he will depart life as he lived it
Doing all that is expected of him. And in this
Final measure he will be missed, his legacy
Secure in the hearts and minds of those he loved.

ii) Matriarchal

For a moment the wistful eyes hold a dreamy
Far-away look a smile as quickly dispels
That lights the still-pleasing face—
In the old photographs she is pretty, and though
By nature disparaging she would deny it,
We too could see what he had seen
Who after all these years still feels the same;
Now the wispy, graying hair frames a face
Figured like a tapestry with the images
Of a lifetime and the lives around which it was
Woven unselfishly, of unfulfilled aspirations—
In the early years, the children and the house
She filled with warmth and love, quietly enjoying
Their triumphs and successes even as she suffered
The defeats and the failures she often could not
Understand, giving to each one in turn something
Of herself and finding there something in return;
She saw her duty clearly and simply and carried it out
Stubbornly through the frailty and the sickness
Complaining no more than most and less
Than she might have of a certain bitterness
And the youth she felt slipping away; their
Needs were simple and they never measured
Happiness by those things she found lacking.
His conscience through the years, she later
Shared his burden of pain and infirmity, reckoning
Then her needs by his who now the world must

View through her eyes, and found at last
A fulfillment of children and grandchildren
And the satisfaction of a lifetime stretching out
Behind her in the union of half a century—
Her duty she might reply, but love to us the same
Just as surely by any other name.

GOING BLIND

Sometimes you can notice it
By the curious way he doesn't look straight
    at you, but askance,
As though he wished to view things from a
    slightly different slant—
Out of the corner of his eye, or the corner
    of his mind, the way
One would at night in looking at a star
Or at some other thing too faint to see, or
    know, straight away;
The center of the retina has deteriorated, the
    images falling there a darkened
Blur of jumbled lines too tangled and distorted
To discern. They have a term for it, these
Medical men who believe that names confer
A measure of understanding: senile macula
    retinitis
And it says nothing. He has his own name
    for it—
It is called going blind, and he understands it
In a way they never will—the sickening sense
    of panic in a
World of early twilights and lingering dawns, the
Fiercely proud spirit helplessly dependent; then
Gradual realization of utter finality. In all
Ten siblings were born—one died a child, another

30

A young man of pneumonia, a third of early
     senility—
The others after sixty-five have all had this
     affliction; now
Three generations of children and grandchildren
Await a fate woven in the twisted strands
     of nucleic acids:
For my part, I shall miss the colors and
The faces of children. But I have seen these
And memory serves me well. More, I would
Crave the sight of words printed boldly on
     smooth pages, for which
The eyes are handmaiden to the mind. Does
This prophecy foretold make each new sunset
Ever more beautiful? It is not possible:
Born with the knowledge of our death, life
     is not sweeter.

I MET A POET

When I was a youth, a poet
Spoke to me, who said:
Poetry is next to godliness—
Beside mathematics and philosophy
And science—
Each thing that we learn
But a tiny part of a greater whole
Expanding without limit
To encompass all knowledge, the universe
And ourselves—
But I paid his words no heed,
Turning from the tortuous twists of poetry
To the plainer paths of science
And spent my years in futile search
Of truth
Ever vanishing into metaphor,
Until lost and confused
I met another poet, who said—
If you would find yourself
Look with the poet's eyes.

TO ALICE WALKER

You stood before us
Alice Walker
wearing jeans and a blouse
the color purple
and quietly read your poems,
and in that hour
I learned as much of poetry
and of passion
as I shall likely ever know;
The color of your skin
Alice Walker
and the proudly braided hair
spoke volumes
of the credibility we also heard
in your words—
about the white though nameless
great-great-grandfather
(Walker, perhaps)
who raped the young slave girl,
and the contempt in your voice
for the jewels
hanging sparkling against Liz's bosom;
And you reminded us
Alice Walker
that there are those who do not love
our wars,
or our governments,
or our riches,
or our values,

or our penises,
but dream their own dreams—
and your words were such we knew
you spoke the truth, and
were ashamed yet glad
it was you we could believe
who told us so;
And there was anger in your words
Alice Walker
and scorn—restrained yet
passionate and not to be denied—
still we did not resent it
but admired you and felt relieved
that you who could tell us
would care enough to try;
And I sat in troubled silence
Alice Walker
of my pen stilled
these many months
and listened to the poems
that touched in me what you had felt
and I have felt before—
and in that hour
you taught me many things,
and I learned as much of poetry
as I shall likely ever know,
but most of all you taught me
Alice Walker
that I care too much
for silence.

HALF-FINISHED POEMS

I have a stack of half-finished poems—
Good beginnings gone awry—most
Beyond repair; beyond redemption, all;
The pen stymied in mid-verse, something
Wrong with each right from the start—
The words flowing out too quickly
Overran the thought, or else labored over
So long the spark extinguished
Before it could be fanned to flames.
Now they lie tucked away in a sheath,
And tucked away in my mind,
Where they will not let me rest
But torment me with their failure
Like stillborn babes, or the anguish
Of a child the parent struggles to save;
Others see the poems but not the labor
And so few words, they think,
Could not cost that much—
They give great pleasure these words of ours
But exact in payment a price of pain
Equal to their bliss.

MONTANA MUSE

Almost overlooked
   in the pale
      moonlight
a small
   hand-lettered sign
      in the window
of the Meagher
   County News
      announcing
"An Afternoon
   of Montana Poetry
      at Chico Hot Springs"
with the date,
   the names
      of a dozen poets
and a special
   invitation for
      certain strangers
like myself
   to join in,
      but unable to
I pass on by,
   later in the
      dark of my room
pleased that
   poetry still lives
      in quiet little

out of the way
        places,
            in the quiet
out of the way
        places
            of the mind.

BREAKDANCING

Every corner
    and the bus stops
        in between
a stage of
    spinning symmetries
        and the choreographed
contortions
    of sinewy shapes
        that spell out
exuberance for life
    and the exultant
        jubilation
of a people
    discovering
        art.

A FULL-TIME OCCUPATION

Writing poems is a full-time occupation;
I don't mean that it pays, and besides
I'd only give the money away, it's best
Done for free; in truth I could not
Do otherwise with no regard to pay
Without dying just a bit and being
Less than the person I still somehow
Need to be. No, it's the evolution
Of the thing, I mean, the ideas come
At the least expected times and in
The least expected ways all bright and full
Of promise and truth that too long neglected
Is never quite the same yet seized upon
Keeps on growing to become more than
At first it seemed revealing truths we did
Not know we knew, "No surprise for
The writer, no surprise for the reader,"
Said Frost, then fixed in thought keeps worrying
Suggesting little changes to my mind
Each one tried against the others to find
That one just right not to disappoint
Till finally set aside to return now and
Then and learn if truth will bear retelling;
Meanwhile the faucets drip the shelves will go
Unfinished, she pretends she does not care
Though at times I know she must; the love

She gives softens here and there a line
That otherwise too harsh might sound for what
Was really meant and harm my purpose; for
The rest they are my own as they must be
It will not work another way. And when
At times my object is the more efficient
Means to kill, though others will not call
It that and say instead to keep the peace,
And anguished faces haunt my mind till I
Grow weary with the world and yearn heartfelt
For other realms which only mind may know,
At length some thought becomes my solace made
A poem, then all else I gladly set
Aside for this my full-time occupation.

A Mystery to Cling To

SEPTEMBER SONG

A ripened harvest moon
Climbs the eastern sky to faintly trace
A rim of mountains
Against the paling night, the geraniums
On my balcony
Show darkly red among the graying leaves,
The cairn McDuff
Keeps his favorite place to watch the
City lights below
Twinkle the silent notes of this September Song;
By day the brilliant
Deep blue skies awash in shimmering light
Reflect in colors
On the earth never clearer in the spring
The season's surge
Of splendor before winter's heavy mantle
Covers all;
Across my shoulder one last trace of day
Gives promise of
The dawn to come and with it hopes
Of one spring more
In the strains of this September Song.

KINGBIRD

The soft
    saffrony
        breast
Flashes
    in the morning sun
        against a grayish
Sculptured
    shape
        perched intently
On the criss-cross
    of wires
        connecting strangers
At their breakfasts;
    dark
        liquid
Orbs
    gleaming brightly
        from the cocked head
Tiny
    convex
        mirrors
To the ebb
    and flow
        of the world below
The vibrant
    form
        darting

Facilely
      flutteringly
            to snare
Prehistoric insects
      above an
            asphalt earth
Struck down
      and mangled
            in the intersection
By the ceaseless
      crush
            of cars
And the people
      going
            nowhere.

STREAMS

Amid purple reflections
    against a stoplight studded
        sky surrounded
By this turbulence
    of clamorous metal bubbles
        relentlessly flowing
In harsh streams—
    am I one of these—
        I am in my presence
Each of us is
    but yet are not
        must not be
To preserve our fragile
    identity
        my own absurdity
Uniquely mine
    disdainful
        scornful of the folly
This aimless senseless
    existence
        intent instead
On bits of captured
    meaning
        that set apart
Still absurdity
    nevertheless
        not unlike in kind

All the other
     even in this the same
        as that
With which
     its purpose
        was to differ.

ON THE TARMAC

All in a row
    towering
        empenages
stretching
    out of a
        primitive past
toward
    a distant
        future
gleaming
    metal tubes
        each
with its
    appendages
        of Hiero's flasks
and fragile
    human cargo
        propelled
on silver sails
    from the
        screech and
roar of this
    technological din
        to the tranquil
obscurity
    of distance
        and time.

A CLOSER WALK
(For DJB)

You walk beside me
Barebreasted in the shimmering sun
Down paths the Anasazi traveled
With mocassined feet—silently, mysteriously—
To a future empty of the sounds
Of laughing brown children, through canyons
Weathered in an ageless earth across
Mesas figured by the sands of time
We, too, marching precariously toward the future—
Building bombs in this desert
And eventually the resolve to unleash them—
Only to foolishly menace ourselves
And our overripe civilization of
Grinning glass and steel thrusting starkly
Above the desert floor, with
Yes, enough to eat but little else
To feed the hunger of souls trapped
Within these barren chasms—
Such now our own truths become
The stern bounty of precious toil
Reaped no more from the land
But from the mind defiantly seduced
Tribute to treacherous gods;
Alongside us
The throaty gurgle of the ever patient river

Its inexorable will staring blankly down
From each cliff face
Heralds the sounds of greater truths where
Few listen and fewer heed—
The tender murmur of ancient sea breezes
Carries the indomitable scream of the red-tail
And the insistent scolding of a marsh wren
To my ears—
The land's truths, not man's
A harsh land indifferent, impartial
Caring as much for these as for man
Who could vanish and the land would not care,
Offering nevertheless clues
Heedless and unheeded
To the riddle of our fate—
And you beside me
Barebreasted in the noonday sun
The clearest vision of all truth
By which we may yet prevail
Where they who walked
These paths before us failed
And vanished.

ALL MY FRIENDS

The knock came gently at the open door:
"Sir," the young man spoke, "I didn't mean
To interrupt..." "Yes, well I am quite busy
Just now," the man responded, "but no, no come
On in," he said and rose to make him welcome;
The tiny office was cluttered with stacks on
Stacks of books, and papers he'd been writing
Scattered across the desk, the words in places
Lined through and written above, some more
     than once
In exacting labor of love. He cleared a chair
Of books and bade him sit; outside the window
A clinging mist hung dangling from the tips of
Jeweled boughs. The man's gaze briefly turned
Back toward the words that he'd been writing;
"My uncle Josh asked me to call," the other
Hastened to explain. "When he learned that
This would be my school, he told me you had
Come here and that I should stop by and say
Hello . . . you do remember Josh and Sarah? . ."
"Why yes, of course," he interrupted, "I should
Have known at once—the freckles and the reddish
Hair—and how are Josh and Sarah? Tell
Me all about them, and about yourself," he
Smiled. "They're fine as near as anyone can
Tell. You know Josh, he's hard to read; never

Complains—just does whatever must be done.
Both mighty sorry to see you go, that much
I know for sure; Josh told me they all were.
Josh says he'll probably never leave. Been
There now for almost thirty years and says
He'll likely stay the rest. I don't suppose
He ever will retire. He told me though to
Tell you that he understands." The young man
Blurted out everything he'd thought of saying.
In his eyes there was the eager look of
Youth the man had come to know and like
In faces all around him. The only hope that's
Left for us, he sometimes told himself. He
Felt anew the empty longing of homesickness
The way he had those first few times he'd severed
Ties and struck out on his own. He didn't
Miss the work. He'd done it for the money
Much longer than he meant to, and for the
Others, and the loyalty and the friendships,
Until he could not do it any more. No,
It was only the people he missed, the ones
Like Josh who understood—him best of all—and
Nothing changed between them. They sat in
    awkward
Silence. "Sir," the youth at length broke in,
"Is something wrong?" "No," he said, "I'm sorry,
It's just that I was thinking—how ironic and
Strange it is—that all my friends build bombs."

THESE OTHERS
(For WCR)

Beside the restless crossroads the little
Cemetery lies silently in the sun
Leeward of a faceless hill cleaved
By the asphalt river linking cities
North and south beneath
A trickle of the flow diverted
East and west to the town
Whose dead here lie in rest;
Interred at last in the universe
Their briefer journey done, impassively
Now they witness the headlong
Rush of others down these paths
To happiness and grief, to love
Hope, despair and deceit, and
Smile knowingly at the heedless
Current streaming ceaselessly by;
Within the trampled, patchwork fence
Nodding weeds adorn unkempt graves
Except here and there where flowers
Show that grief is new or memory
Strong and death an ever deepening
Mystery to those whose lives it
Harshly touched and forever changed;
Broken headstones and whitewashed
Markers stand aslant or lie tumbled

In the weeds between the graves
Decaying in the sun and rain the relentless
Dissolution of death, silently
Mocking those passing in review;
These oblivious to lessons written
In the earth rush hurriedly
By loath to pause and view
Graves lying idly in the sun,
Shunning to acknowledge the greater
Significance of the peaceful little
Cemetery than the delicate veil
Of weeds draped lightly across
The arid hills, grasping instead
Tenaciously at life as though
Embracing death were the final
Defeat, unmindful that all journeys
Must end here to begin anew; these others,
Sleeping silently against the turmoil
Of the ages, merely smile,
Seeing all is the same
And knowing it is good.

THAT LARGER RIDDLE

Behold
the bountiful apple tree, singular among
those others on my morning walk whose
seeds become but useless litter for the
gardener's rake among these too neat plots

with its burgeoning burden of bright green
globes, the succulent seed casings that blush
and sweeten in the autumn sun to be picked
in anticipation beforehand from the bough
or fall unnoticed thuddingly to the ground

and eaten, or lie neglected somewhere in the
slackening sun to soften and decay in fragrant
ferment either way the seeds discarded and
dispersed to find new expression in wood and fruit
and flower of living tree and wonderment

of how it ever came to be, in what way
and how many centuries upon fathomless aeons
germ cells came to know the greater purpose
of the tree, not a feat to be demeaned and
dismissed as but the labor of seven days

nor have we in our fanciful musings got it
right, but unresolvable mystery to ones

constrained to measure time in numbered days and
years and patience measured in restraint too
feckless to stay the murderer's hand, and if not

this simpler puzzle of a tree, how then to
know that larger riddle of you and me.

McDUFF

Gradually in the quickening light
He edges ever closer
To wake me,
The eager tongue gently
Licking my face and exploring
The offered hand,
Welling anticipation
Spilling over into nervous whines,
Then the obsequious gestures—
Paws and soft underbelly
Thrust upward, fawning,
Imploring me
To our morning run
On this the rarest of mornings
With its extra edge—
A light rain waters
The desert floor and
Dull gray clouds cling
To nocturnal snow
Shrouding the foothills nearby—
As if he too senses
The shortening span
Of days loathe
To relinquish a single one,
And escaping our gift of reason
With its endless questions
Has his own exuberant philosophy

Of the senses,
Impatient as always
This rarest of mornings
To put it into practice.

.

CHRISTMAS EVE

Life is full of courage
turning me shamefaced
from my cares—
This morning
an old woman huddled
in the pre-dawn chill
waiting for a bus,
At noon a worn gaunt
figure scavenging food
from the garbage wearing
gloves not to soil
his hands,
This evening in the shops
a ragged anxious
mother tenderly consoling
her disappointed child—
Overhead in the night
sky a white bird soaring
on the city lights—
Later in my room
on the other side of night
never such outpouring
of hope
from Greek heroic hexameters.

A MYSTERY TO CLING TO

Along the firm unyielding sand
At water's edge I run
Through rain and failing light
Into the darkness, the sun's
Last rays across my shoulders
Draped against the night,
The raindrops falling gently
At the start, pelting angrily,
Impede my progress. Shorebirds
And the gulls ignore
My passage as though one
Drenched and darkly cloaked
Were a kindred thing;
Thirsty tongues of lightning
Lap the tops of waves
Far out to sea, the flickering
Light showing up the scene
Like the staccato strum
Of memory, startling me;
A crashing clap of thunder
Frightens and I flinch sideways,
Then amused, wonder why—
Isn't it merely to survive,
To try to be a part of all this
For as long as I can; to
Ponder endless questions without
Answers, and for what purpose?

This giant seeing eye so
Vast the mind cannot conceive
Can have no regard for man.
It cannot matter, I think,
Yet know it does and
Speaks to something deep inside
Perhaps a thing apart
From all this other—
It is a mystery to cling to
Till the last breath.
The danger fills me
With a delicious joy
Of what it means to be alive
Now, at this moment, as I
Make my way down the beach
Dodging thunderclaps in the rain.

ON VIEWING THE IMPRESSIONISTS

i)   Quiet serious Monet
    discussing art with Pissarro
    at the Cafe Guerbois or
    the scoffing sensitive Renoir,
    more likely listening
    to Zola or Degas
    with Sisley
    and the ill-fated Bazille,
    escaping to the country
    to paint in
    sumptuous floods of light the
    short choppy strokes
    and bright daubs
    of color
    —too much garish color, they cried—
    arrayed separately
    on the canvas for the eye
    to combine in scenes
    of the only
    truth he saw
    —unacceptable for the Salon, they ruled,
    no substance nothing
    of the mind's eye—
    in images blurred like
    captured motion or a world
    taking form
    to as quickly fade from view

—not truly paintings at all,
they argued, too unreal
merely impressions—
yes, that was it
impressions
of a reality
ever shrinking
to exactly fit
these frames.

ii) Explaining it all
    years later to the five sons
    Pissarro the astute
    elder and many ways their leader
    —a man worth consulting, said
    Cezanne, and something like God Himself—
    who understood Monet
    and the new Impressionism
    not impressions
    but reality itself depicted
    as the senses
    in *plein-air* colors
    and softly smeared perceptions,
    taking his lead from
    the new Heraclitus but holding
    to the clearer colors
    and surer shapes of his early years
    —you are a great blunderer, Sir,
    wrote Zola,
    you are an artist that I like—
    to fashion his own reality,
    not of forms
    but the feelings
    captured on each canvas.

iii)   Renoir who
        scoffed at theories
        painting was for pleasure
        —if it didn't amuse me
        then I shouldn't paint, he said—
        found in fragile colors
        and softly muted shapes that
        display the delicate touch
        striving for a time
        with his friend Monet
        after the new
        realism, then
        tiring rejected it
        for the tender
        sensuous faces of
        women and children,
        to paint reality
        peering
        demurely back.

iv)   Sisley at Marley
       Bazille's *Beach at Sainte Adresse*
       the triumphs went
       unnoticed, one
       neglected the
       other a soldier's
       grave: impressions
       of the reality
       of us
       all.

POPPA

He dogged my footsteps throughout
The city
       past the booksellers' stalls
Along the quais to a good cafe on
The Place St-Michel
          the shadowy
Barrel-chested figure hands thrust
Into pockets head bowed graying
Hair and beard deepening winter's
Chill
      through the Luxembourg Gardens
Past Gertrude Stein's and 113 rue
Notre-Dame-des-Champs to the bustling
Closerie des Lilas
           all traces
Have vanished
         at 74 rue du
Cardinal Lemoine a discotheque
Replaces the sawmill, the voices
Of the charmed circle strangely
Silent at 27 rue de Fleurus
            only
The books survive and the few
Truths
       was it the early ones
When he first got lucky full of
Raw exuberance for life or the last
Ones wiser more compassionate and

Revealing
                    and the one about this
Place in the early years many ways
Closest to the truth
                              I caught a
Glimpse in the Jeu de Paume the
Figure hunched intently before a canvas
Studying Cezanne to learn about
Writing
                    and in a clean well-lighted
Cafe the saucers stacked high pouring
Over yesterday's words to see if they
Were still true
                         once during dinner
At the Polidor listening and thinking
About what he wanted to do with
Conversations
                    nowhere yet everywhere
The watchful figure
                         among the crowds
On windswept streets and lovers in the
Gardens, in the cafes and the shops—
Anywhere there was life, that truth he
Found here and made his own—
                                   life and
Death and courage
                         summer and winter
And spring
              and always the promise

Of another spring whispered from every
Stone and gray-green chestnuts beside
The Seine—
                    courage for our time.

THE WRITER

At the pinnacle of his powers he suddenly
Blew his brains out one night with both
Barrels of a favorite Holland and Holland
Double rifle which he himself had used
In Africa for close work in heavy cover
While engaged as always in living the
Image he created in his writing and
Gathering the inspiration that sustained
Him, until in dying by his own hand he
Seemingly confounded those who felt they
Knew him because of those same writings
And who believed that the image and
His last act were somehow irreconcilable;
But in reality the image explains the act,
Not one of desperation but the willful
Deliberate decision to control his fate,
To choose the time and circumstances
Of the inevitable and escape the slow decay
And long dissolution of his powers that
Was just beginning, and to manifest
In this final gesture the same courage
He had lived by and which he had
Written into the image because it
Was an inseparable part of his nature;
The unmistakable signs of it were there
In the last books he wrote but never
Lived to see published, in which he revealed
More of himself and the man behind the
Image than he had in any of the others,

And in so doing finally discovered
Regret the way previously he had
Discovered pity in writing the best book
Till then, and in living it through
Writing about it made it his own
And inscribed it into the image;
During his life he had known but
Never written of depression and despair,
So he chose a moment of happiness
When life was sweetest as his moment
Of death, taking charge of his own
Destiny after the manner of so many
Of his characters, choosing from among
The weapons in his collection the one
He deemed most worthy of the task,
Putting the cold barrels in his mouth
And pulling the triggers himself at
The end of a pleasant evening because
He knew life could never be sweeter,
And because he more than anyone
Understood that longer is not better
But merely longer, and because as
Always he never lacked the will or
The courage to live life to the fullest
Even at the blinding instant of death.

PEACEMAKER

The hard, shiny barrel had worn dull and satiny
    from the caresses of too many admirers and
The stropping of holsters whose oil-soaked
    leathers molded to its shape, wore through
And were discarded; the first had been a
    patriarch in whose hands the .45 Colt became
An extension of his nature, killing in a barroom
    brawl a drunken Indian who wanted killing
And then another who didn't and yet another
    until wrested from his grip it killed him
Horribly in the eye the brains splattered on the
    sawdust-littered floor
For the liver-coated cur to lap; wrapped
In a woolen blanket, standard army issue,
    shielded from the woman's disapproving scrutiny
It went by mule at the bottom of a cedar trunk
    north to the Platt River
And on a flatboat to the Missouri arriving by
    barge in St. Louis a fortnight later
With the son and young wife and boy to be
Carried by steamer down the great river to
    New Orleans where a square-rigged schooner
Took it on the spice run to Boston and the
    small mercantile business purchased
With the last savings of the patriarch in a poor
    Irish neighborhood; gunning down
A few months later the slender nervous youth
    who

Attempted to rob the scant silver coins that
  were all the register ever held
The shots coming in anger and frustration at
  the gnawing failure that had
Slowly robbed the man of spirit and pride and
  dignity and finally of life itself
At the hands of an angry mob in revenge for
  the senseless killing; enraged by
Her grief the woman entrusted the gun to the
  boy's uncle who instead kept it safely
Hidden for the time when the boy would
  become a man, carrying it himself up
San Juan Hill in Cuba in '98 and firing it that
  day until the barrel was too hot to hold
Emptying the bandoliers draped across his chest
  and a cartridge belt as well never knowing
The outcome the boy never tiring of hearing his
  uncle recount it; claiming it
At last for his own when his mother died and
  still only a boy carried it
With him to the trenches in France in '17
  firing it just once and then
To end the piteous cries of a gunner whose face
  was blown away a living
Corpse begging through the night for the
  merciful gift of death; after the war
With no appetite left for killing putting it away
  for more than twenty years

At the bottom of a dresser drawer wrapped in
    oily linen inside a holster with
A button-down flap, taking it out once to
    register it with the town sheriff
And again after a mob had lynched a black man
    and set fire to the corpse
Then to reassure his wife but instead frightening
    her and the Negro servants who would
Not return to work until the gun was safely
    hidden, and once for each
Of the three sons to teach them in turn to fire
    it because he knew
They could not avoid learning anyway and
    because he hoped to endow it
With a solemnity that would render it neither
    game nor sport but a responsibility
To be exercised with a discretion mature
    beyond their years; the oldest
Claiming the right to wear it ashore at
    Normandy and through the French countryside
In that same button-down holster firing it only
    to shoot hares in the moonlight
Along the banks of canals where the Germans
    had retreated, each
Silhouetted form shot carefully through the
    head and skinned and dressed to be
Cooked and eaten for breakfast or traded for
    cigarettes and privileges, the pistol

Otherwise worn mainly for luck, losing it once in a
  game of poker
To an infantryman who goaded him into betting it
  against a sure thing
And then refused to sell it back, returned by a
  superstitious corpsman after
The soldier was killed, going twenty miles out of his
  way and narrowly escaping
Himself when a bullet smashed the windshield of his
  jeep,
For a time giving it to a woman with whom he had
  stayed for three weeks
Teaching her to use it against her fear of abuse if the
  Germans returned
But taking it with him when he left haunted by the
  faces of the two small children
And afraid of what the woman might do, wearing it
  finally into Paris but no further,
Word coming that his father was dying and he
  furloughed back to the States
And eventually out of the service; as the eldest
Claiming the pistol for his own the new bride sternly
  disapproving
But he adamant then putting it away for good at her
  insistence
In the top drawer of that same dresser where it lay
  hidden for years
Under the clean white handkerchiefs and boxes of
  ties to be discovered occasionally

By prying eyes that only sensed what lay wrapped
   in the smooth linen
Beneath the stiff flap of the new holster; the proud
   youth one afternoon
Secretly showing the twin sister the forbidden
   treasure lovingly unwrapped it
To hold the smooth handle in both hands the
   hammer pulled slowly back
Slipping from beneath his thumb the bullet striking
   the girl in the face and
Killing her even before the sound had died in his
   ears; afterwards
The pistol disappeared the man and the woman each
   believing that the other
Had taken it neither caring anymore the woman
   blaming him and he
Blaming himself and unable to live with it gradually
   destroying them all, until now,
Where it lies on the attic floor beside the spreading
   pool of blood and
The lifeless body of the quiet, sensitive young man.

THE BALLAD OF BOBBIE'S BUCKEYE BAR
(For GWS)
With Apologies to Robert W. Service

From out of the desert they came by two's
In their drab gray government cars
In search of a glass of ice cold brew
At Bobbie's Buckeye Bar.

They spent their days below the ground
In tunnels men had made
The reasons hushed, though the rumor going round
Said they did it for the shade.

The sun now spent hung low in the slack
A bulging bloodshot eye
Peering aslant at that clapboard shack
Where this night a woman would try.

The moon rose up in the east pale gold
To shine on the scene below
Where in years to come the tale would be told
Of how Slim had just said no.

There was Shorty and Slim, the others and Rojo
And they came with a thirst to quench
But they reckoned without this gal named Flo
Who some say was a winsome wench.

She took an immediate hankering to Slim
And joined them at the bar
Taking her place in the space by him
This fair-haired desert star.

She touched his cheek and twirled his hair
And gently rubbed his back
And tried to get him to follow her there
To her room at the rear of the shack.

She nuzzled his neck and nipped his ear
And whispered things to him
That were spoken too low for the others to hear
She meant them only for Slim.

She looked in his eyes and stroked his chest
To the others it was more than clear
What they would do away from the rest
In the dark of her room at the rear.

She leaned right over to give him a peek
At a bosom that amply showed
Hers was no game of hide and seek
But a gift she freely bestowed.

She talked to him in a constant purr
Of the things that they would do
And of how if he would follow her
She could make him feel like new.

But through it all this hero just stood
And slowly sipped his beer
And thought of how she would be good
And wished that he wasn't here.

And even today in the Buckeye Bar
The patrons tell this tale
Of the tall dark man in the government car
To whom Flo couldn't make a sale.

Till when at last he turned to leave
There was not a dry eye in the place
The restraint of this fellow they couldn't believe
And tears wet every face.

He paused there a moment to slip a ten
In the center of Flo's brassiere
And caught the tremor of quivering chin
As she whispered in his ear.

And those who said they could hear the words
She spoke so soft and mellow
Swear that what they thought they heard
Was a sad "So long, big fellow."

O LITTLE FLOWER
(For RDG)

O little flower
     your
Petals pink and red
     atop
The young green stalk
     nurtured
In the soil misfortune tilled
     and watered
With the tears of joy and sorrow
     till
Plucked and taken from me
     by one
Herself that parting could not bear
     to grow
In ways unseen I may never know
     and though
Apart O little flower
     you
Are in my thoughts always
     and none
Will ever love you more
     than me
O little flower.

DEJA VU

The son I fathered when I was barely
His age was just here and left
With someone now that he loves
To drive through the night and the
Next day and night to a school
Where the likes of him should be—
Bright, eager, curious—the final hope
Of what we and our kind have wrought,
And to the still segregated society where he
Soon will learn whatever of justice and
    compassion
One can know. We are different, I think,
And yet the same; he has his mother's
Softness but in him I imagine I see
The seeds of all I have become
And would share what I have found
But know he must discover it for himself
Or heed it not. And we turn apart,
I to live one truth at a time
Between now and the end, he
To assault the future with the
Hopes and options of youth, and
We are both right; my way will not
Work now for him nor his any longer for
Me. In my love I wish for him far better
Than I have known, but in my anxiety
For the dangers looming ahead and
In the truths I have found, I know,
That I may only hope it can be as good.

MARY, MARY

Somewhere in the darkness of amniotic
Night the tiny beating heart stopped
Imperceptible in the city's throbbing
Pulse, dawn brings the gushing currents of cars,
Again at sunset, the people like marionettes
Dangling at the ends of strings hapless;
What will he think she wondered when she learned
Grieving for them both but young in his faith
He simply took it for the best; she thought
It was too easy to dismiss this unborn
Being no one had known but her and she
But little, even the moment of death and instant
Of conception unmemoried against the future—
The foetus in the womb two months before
She knew, the death at first unnoticed in
The bustle of her life then stillborn labor
And it was ended in simple ritual and things
That must get done, she had no choice but live
Each moment as it came, the hours then
The days dragging her along in their embrace
Wresting from her grasp the meaning that
She sought, until once more the beauty of
Each day, the peaceful little cemetery,
The soothing words the kindly cleric spoke
All began to dull the knife edge of her
Pain; she did not want to be consoled—

The fanciful reasons men have always used
To mask their fears when needed most are not
Enough, it is too easy she thought, without
The hurt the meaning would be lost, the questions—
At times she thought she saw the answers in
The blaze and twinkle of the city's lights,
Night is when it's most alive she thought,
Darkness lets us be ourselves; though mindless
From afar, she felt the meaning in its
Throbbing pulse and heard again the questions:
The questions are the only truth, she thought—
The questions are their own best answers, she knew.

83

TO A DAUGHTER

Do not be
    distressed
        by the sadness
I thought
    I saw
        in your eyes
or by the urge
    you sometimes have
        to cry;
it is all
    a part
        of being human
that none
    of us
        escapes—
without which
    the joy
        and the happiness
would also
    lose
        their meaning.

HOMEWARD BOUND

Out the window
    of a passing car
        a pretty girl
hails:
    I LIKE your LEGS
        and, self-consciously, the
tired pace quickens
    fatigue forgotten
        the remaining distance
conquered effortlessly,
    vainly; that night
        behind drawn shades
I whirl and dance
    in giddy celebration
        of these old legs
which have come
    so far, so
        many miles to go.

2/1/40

Forty-five years ago today,
Barely half of the ninety
I wish that I might live
On such a day as this,
Bitter cold then too, as now
A world white and full of wonder
Every birth its own miracle—
Mine and hers and later
Those of the children,
Like all the children everywhere,
What happens afterward separates us
Scattered across the gulf of years lost
Beyond the reach of reason
Each in his own way
To see it through, with
A curiosity at times grown morbid
At the gnawing realization of the truth,
Only the details obscure
The pattern laid out clearly before us
For all to confront—
This the real meaning of honesty,
No longer any comfort but a sense
Of betrayal in pretense and denial;
Can the wonderment survive such scrutiny
Or must every reality flounder
On its own frailty?

I would have my life end amidst
The frenzied renewal of some distant spring
Supplanting winter's slumber
Merely one more event in a cycle
Of endless change,
No more certain of any purpose
To be sure, but still rejoicing
In the boundless mysteries of why.

MOTES

The awning
left
a space

that sunlight
filled
about which

a demanding
woman
complained her

table heaped
with
food but

another across
the
way deferred

saying there
were
worse things

than sunlight
in
her eyes.

REASONS ENOUGH

Waking
in the half light I feel
your softness
pressing my length and
haltingly grope
to find your mouth,
the warm scent of your breath
stirring a new
awakening

Before last night
I did not even know you—
tomorrow
for us both may dim
the memory,
there are things between
us that will go unsaid, but
for now I caress you
with all the generosity
of my being—

You, too, are kind

The singing of the bed
the picture on your wall
a nude reclining
on a quilt, art
suddenly close to truth,

intrude upon my
thoughts—

Your tenderness, this yearning
the unrestrained intimacy, the
overwhelming sense of sharing—
reasons
enough for this moment,
or for a lifetime.

THE LESSON

What are you reading?
I had not seen her for a week;
Darling, she said,
I found this wonderful new writer
Who is very good—
I don't know,
But everything he says just seems
So right to me—
I smiled and was glad,
Truth never more clearly captured
By innocence, I thought,
And suddenly
It seemed so right to me.

5/10/85

It has the sound of a good
Beginning, she persisted,
And when you write it—5/10/85—
There is a solid look about it—
A respectable number, and most
Auspicious. The Greeks would much
Have preferred something with a 4
Or perhaps a 7, I teased—
Too conservative, everything evenly divisible
By 5, the sum of the first two numbers
Exactly the difference between the third
And a century; viewed as a fraction
Completely rational; besides, 3 would be
More symbolic and mystical—
The maitre d' had reservations
Available for the 9th, but she
Remained insistent—9 would be as
Many times more magic, I continued,
Being 3^2, and anyway it really all
Began four years ago, on a 27th
I believe. The Greeks would have
Found the 10 perfection, she objected,
And 5 half of perfection; can you
Imagine being married on the 17th
Or the 23rd, or—so ordinary,
Nothing to distinguish it. We cannot

Choose what day we are born, nor
For most the time of death, or how
Pretty or intelligent or fortunate—
So little is ours to determine—but
Here, where we can choose, and
So much depending on the outcome;
She wrote it out again—5/10/85—
It will command respect down through
The years, she added;
It is so hard to know how things
Will work, or what will happen—
We deserve the best beginning;
Hush, I said, and placed my finger
On her lips. Everything will work out
Fine—I've known it all along—
Not because of any special day,
But just because you're you—
And because that you would want
To choose—5/10/85.

Heed the Voices of Anger

In the desert
I saw a creature, naked, bestial,
Who, squatting upon the ground,
Held his heart in his hands,
And ate of it.
I said: "Is it good, friend?"
"It is bitter—bitter," he answered;
"But I like it
Because it is bitter,
And because it is my heart."

Stephen Crane

THE PRICE WE PAY

There is a mindlessness that wasn't there
Before—Is it what Lucretius felt
What resigned Thoreau to an early
Death, or am I only losing patience?
Had you known me before you wouldn't
Think so, then perhaps I could convince you
Of my apprehension and share these fears;
Outside my window it is raining
And the afternoon is gray, winter
Has settled over the desert,
Dark clouds rim the mountains
Against the city—yet it is not gloomy
But beautiful and deeply reassuring,
Its purpose fulfilled in its own being—
Only man senses the absurdity
And alone suffers for his intellect:
It is, after all, merely the price we pay
For our meaning.

HEED THE VOICES OF ANGER

Whereto the runes of reason:
With them Socrates conquered the Dionysian
    spirit and disillusioned,
Athens pointed to distant decline;
Lucretius composed for troubled minds but
    Rome unsoothed
Plunged the world to darkness;
Briefly like a meteor the Age of Reason lit up
    the western world—
Voltaire poured out his heart exhausted
In the folly of empire; and we but a passing
    phase to
Something else too ominous to contemplate—
At such times heed the voices of anger, the
    cries of
Caring, passionate poets too full
Of love for restraint—Euripides, Nietzsche,
    Thoreau, Jeffers—
Their pages stained with angry tears;
Our world smolders like a buried ember
    needing only
A breath of air and we numbed
Silence our fears and speak of baseball and
    politics and greed—
Let us raise a shout of anger!

ECCE HOMO

The slight little man with the nervous
Stomach and weak eyes,
To those few who inquired deferential to
A fault
Yet railing mightily against his demons
Through
Nine volumes wrenched from the depths
Of his solitude—
I am so completely alone, he would write,
Then—
Ariadne, I love you—and a date with
Madness—
What price this genius that gives our
Souls such pleasure—
What price Faulkner's suffering
Camus' godless anguish
Nietzsche's madness
To give our hearts such hope?

TOR HOUSE FESTIVAL

The great man is dead now—for God's sake
Let him be—
Where were we when it could have made
A difference:
Though he likely never would acknowledge it
Who knows
What solace he might have found in the
Slightest kindness
Withheld against the storms of scorn weathered
By his art?
Now it is too late—this is only for us
Not him—
What would he think: this place, these people
Our times
A teeming testament to all he held suspect
But inevitable?
He, instead, would have us suffer in silence
The lessons
He taught than to celebrate them to some
Empty purpose.

A CONCISE CHRONOLOGY OF WESTERN ART

Prehistoric
Egyptian, Greek, Roman
Medieval, Byzantine, Gothic
Renaissance
Baroque, Rococo, Neo-Classical
Romanticism, Impressionism
Expressionism, Surrealism, Cubism
Abstraction—
Genius depicting the world
Each in its turn
In the truths of its time,
The soul crying out in rapture
And in anguish to be
Held up to our eyes as a mirror
No truth everlasting—
And what of our time, are we
To believe the prophecy
Of its harsh unfeeling abstraction
A future devoid of humanity,
The way difficult and fraught
With peril?
It, too, is a truth to be replaced.

TO THE OPTIMIST

To the optimist I would say: we take too much
   pride in our maimed and killed and missing,
The young men sent to do old men's bidding
To break women's and children's hearts for
   reasons too much rhetoric: the first time
Was for freedom and a new nation built upon
Shining principles tarnished by the sweat of
   slavery and brothers' blood at places with
Names like Shiloh and Antietam and
   The Wilderness;
And this century: "the war to end all wars"
   and then the next "to make the world safe
For democracy" and the next and the next each
   more vivid
In the images of its horrors, chisled with civic
   pride everlastingly into mute monuments
To those who sacrificed and were slaughtered; they
Are blameless—they merely did what they did—
   we embrace the guilt: our politicians
Speak too glibly of these with overweening pride and
Slogans to shutter the light of reason; yes, there
   is evil in the world and principle at times
The proper conscience of practice, when men
    must do
What they must do—but to relish it and glorify
   it—that is the difference—that which
Makes you the optimist, and me to wonder why.

FALKLANDS

It is winter and war has come to
These islands:
Across storm-tossed seas corrupt Britannia
Strutting vaingloriously
One final moment in the sun sends warships
Against petty little dictators
The sons of honest folk in the balance;
No honor here—only equal wrongs—
America which neither side could oppose
Heaps rhetoric from afar upon graves
Of Argentine youth—
As a war it is of no real consequence
Merely a minor skirmish,
More penguins than people will perish,
An ad for Exocets and Entendards and
Good for the world's economy, more jobs
For French farmers—
Can we ever hope to build these weapons
Without using them?
No one should believe it.

WHAT DIFFERENCE?

With numbing roar a bomb explodes in roiling
    clouds of dust and smoke
And piercing bits of shrapnel that maim
And kill: two hundred marines, a busload
    of children
The detested "Brit"—the design of fanatical
Desperate men—and outraged we condemn
    the act as
Barbarous, secure in moral indignation; yet
We are just such terrorists, more sophisticated
    perhaps in coat and tie
Dealing death by formulae articulated in
Fanciful metaphors, but holding the world
    nevertheless hostage
To gain our ends: peace and freedom we call it
To fix the blame elsewhere, still the outcome
    will be the same
Ourselves the object of our own terror:
What difference threatening the destruction of
    the planet or merely
Killing a few innocent people?

BUT REMEMBER—THIS IS AMERICA

The controversy rages on both sides
Of the globe, across war-memoried
Europe at Russia's doorstep,
In the Kremlin and the White House,
A contest of will for supremacy
Easily resolved by simply counting:
Which side has the most warheads—
One side thirty thousand, the other
Perhaps a few more or less—
Ah, but there is the matter of which has
The greater capability strategic and tactical
First strike, second strike, strategies
For denial of victory and even winning,
Besides, the numbers lie and emotions
Are what count here;
Fools—One thousand are enough
To destroy this fragile patchwork
We call civilization and plunge
The world into a gloom of nuclear winter
Filled with cries of starving children
Hollow-eyed, shivering, bellies distended,
With running sores no way to end
Their suffering but death;
Yes, but remember—this is America, and
We must be first in everything
Including the means to destroy the earth.

107

A CHILD'S METAPHOR

One
tiny
drop
of
rain
after
another
through this graying mist,
in spring
the rivers overflow—
one
faltering
step
of
mankind
after
another
through this deepening gloom,
in winter
the graves overflow.

CIRCA 1984

We are very sorry, it began,
cannot offer you the position . . .
. . . credentials . . . impressive . . .
certain you are well qualified to teach
however . . . found the statement of your
religious beliefs unacceptable . . .
That still—after how many centuries
Unable to face our doubts without the
Old fears and hatreds, the predatory
Rooted instincts for survival—cannot
Every man yet proclaim with Nietzsche
From any street corner that God is
Dead without the others noticing or
Have we in truth learned nothing
Before or since? All around our horizons
Men cower in fear and isolation
At other men's convictions—
Weak, paranoid creatures unsuited for
Survival. Before, we killed for food,
Clothing, shelter—to exist. Now
Civilized, we murder with consuming
Sophistication for our beliefs—
To perish.

TO IMAGINED GODS

This may yet
Be our greatest shame: Palestinians
Displaced to redress Nazi horrors
And salve the conscience of a guilt-tormented
World; and for what
Purpose? Because the ancient parchments
Proclaimed it as prophecy? And what
Of Mohammed? What of every zealot who claims
To hear the voice of God
Demanding bloody penance? Is there
To be no end of our folly
Or the pain and suffering we would inflict
In obeisance
To imagined Gods?

LET US PRAY

The plains of Persia bear the stench of bodies
    rotting in the sun—for
Jihad and the wrath of the Ayatollah;
Behind the Star of David and the ancient
    prophecy of Kings
Israelis cower in terror of car bombs and
Make war on their neighbors; the Moral
    Majority defends the morality of
Nuclear weapons, and seeks to deny as unholy
Abortion, and the right of women to free choice;
An aging President, firm in his faith, discusses
    with friends
Nuclear holocaust as the long awaited fulfillment
Of Revelation in our time; the masses,
    frightened, turn to fatalism
Or to prayer—Let us all join with them
And pray devoutly for Godless leaders.

THE GREAT DEBATE

Do we demand such ambition of them
These politicians
That they hold no place for honor but
Only lie and lie
While we, wishing to believe, gullibly
Lap it up
Like some cringing cur greedily gobbling
Its own vomit—
Can there be any surprise that no one
Recognizes truth,
Or that they treat us with contempt
As fools?
Where are our great leaders, our own
Lucius Quinctius Cincinnatus,
Our Lincoln, or were these too merely
More lies?

THE EMPEROR'S NEW CLOTHES

Aging,
This President stands before us looking
Youthful and vigorous
And speaks in honeyed phrases that soothe
And reassure,
The old deceptions heard in every age—
Of greed and disregard—
To ears too eager to believe; not even
A child to warn them
That like all the others before, these
Are not new clothes—
Merely another naked emperor.

GIVE ME IRON MEN

Give me iron men and iron mountains
The poet's plea—
They have always imagined it so—
And history has answered
With men who have made a difference
Both good and evil, yet
Always with manageable consequence;
These new tools will change that
And we shall not think them
Iron men, but pitiful, dying
With the rest, whining and sniveling
In floods of excrement from loosened bowels.

The Poet's Last Wish

ONE SPRING MORE

So much to say
    so little time
        so many ways
To say it
    how is it no one
        wants to hear
These sounds
    leaves cascading silently
        under autumn's pressing burden
Minstrels of the season
    on every path abound
        faces turned to rain-soaked
Trunks
    gray flannel oaks
        softly dripping promise
Yet another spring
    and another
        and another
Till it ends
    for each of us
        and then for all
If ever
    can it really matter when
        or how
These stones
    cold smooth dumb
        and frozen lumps

Of clay
    forever swirling round
        a world
Neither void
    nor matter
        but both
And mindless mystery besides
    if then
        why not now
Birds
    flowers
        if viewed
Too closely
    mirror this mystery
        and everything falls apart
We must believe it
    already we treat it
        so
Just one more spring
    we hope
        and follow winter's progress
Yet will not hear
    the warnings
        clearer than these
Damp earth
    and rocks
        thrust aside

By the budding crocus
    soft warm winds
        sigh
The sounds
    of our relief
        this one spring more.

ROWAN OAK

Rowan Oak stands empty—silent
Like its master—
Veiled in gray despair of deepening December dusk
    and
The verdant decadence of untended cedar
And magnolia—
A haunting melancholy stares from its darkened
    windows
Like his sorrowful eyes
That moved the playwright to tears

Mostly neglected—
Like he was in his lifetime
There are still those here who would like to
    forget
Few have read even one of the books
He gave his life to
Or ever paused to wonder why it mattered—
Honored and acclaimed he had by then
Poured out his soul too often
And the scars ran deep

A poet he called himself—
Not for the failed volumes of poetry
But a spiritual kinship with
Homer and Aeschylus and Euripides
A writer's writer—they knew

So much talent, warned Sherwood Anderson,
    if you aren't
Careful you won't write anything
Hemingway for his short stories, said
    Steinbeck, but
Faulkner for anything he ever wrote—
The best we have had—
He wrote with his heart on his sleeve
Such consuming passion only genius could
    sustain—
"A life's work in the agony and sweat of the
Human spirit," he would say in Stockholm, ". . .
About the human heart in conflict with
Itself which alone can make good writing
Because only that is worth writing about,
Worth the agony and the sweat"—
And they knew

He became this place—
Jefferson and Yoknapatawpha County along the
Tallahatchie River—
Compson's Mile, Sutpen's Hundred
The Big Woods—
Waystops on a chart of the imagination,
His own little postage stamp of native soil
    so rich
He could never live long enough to exhaust it
And didn't—
In the years since

Faulkner country has changed
And is changeless
Having passed to the trust of others who will
Make of it what they will
But can never erase the words
By which he made it his

Now a generation has passed—
Another generation lived in the constant
        realization
We could all be blown up
And the words take on new significance— "I
decline to accept the end of man," he had said,
"I believe that man will not merely endure:
He will prevail."
And in that, the poet's last wish
And greatest promise—
Such men peer deeply, passionately
And we may hope with clearer vision
Though others would disagree;
Behind the veil of gray despair that dusk has drawn
This place is strangely silent
And empty
The words but fading echoes in the stillness
As I strain to hear the poet's last wish
And turn again
Toward one spring more.